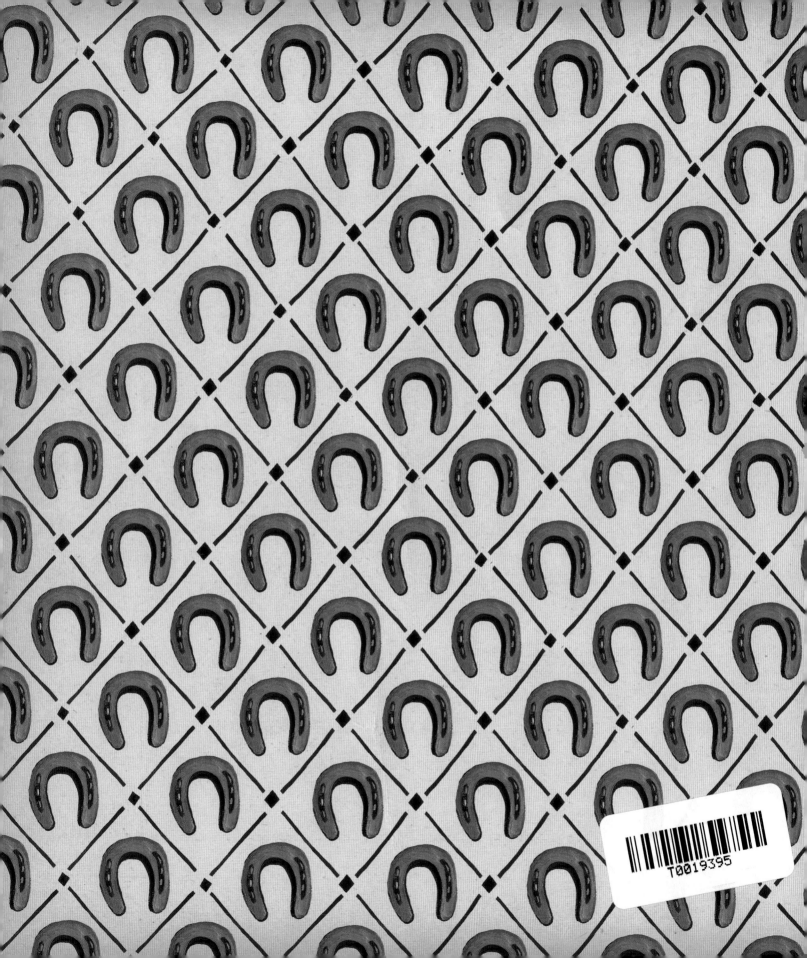

SIMON & SCHUSTER BOOKS FOR YOUNG READERS

An imprint of Simon & Schuster Children's Publishing Division

1230 Avenue of the Americas, New York, New York 10020

© 2008 by Meghan McCarthy

Book design by Jessica Handelman © 2008 by Simon & Schuster, Inc.

SIMON & SCHUSTER BOOKS FOR YOUNG READERS

and related marks are trademarks of Simon & Schuster, Inc.

For information about special discounts for bulk purchases, please contact Simon & Schuster

Special Sales at 1-866-506-1949 or business@simonandschuster.com.

The Simon & Schuster Speakers Bureau can bring authors to your live event.

For more information or to book an event, contact the Simon & Schuster Speakers Bureau

at 1-866-248-3049 or visit our website at www.simonspeakers.com.

Also available in a Simon & Schuster Books for Young Readers hardcover edition

The text for this book was set in Century 731 BT.

The illustrations for this book were rendered in acrylic paint.

Manufactured in China

0423 SCP

First Simon & Schuster Books for Young Readers paperback edition April 2021

2 4 6 8 10 9 7 5 3

The Library of Congress has cataloged the hardcover edition as follows:

McCarthy, Meghan.

Seabiscuit the wonder horse / Meghan McCarthy.—1st ed.

p. cm.

"A Paula Wiseman Book."

ISBN 978-1-4169-3360-1 (hardcover)

ISBN 978-1-5344-9577-7 (pbk)

1. Seabiscuit (Racehorse)—Juvenile literature. 2.—Racehorses—
United States—Biography—Juvenile literature. 3. Horse
racing—United States—Juvenile literature. I. Title.

SF355.S4M33 2008

798.40092'9—dc22

2008006729

Seabiscuit
~the~
Wonder Horse

Meghan McCarthy

A PAULA WISEMAN BOOK

SIMON & SCHUSTER BOOKS FOR YOUNG READERS

New York London Toronto Sydney

In the 1930s, times were tough. There were long lines to get food. People didn't have much and needed an escape.

Going to the racetrack was the perfect escape.
People came from far and wide to watch their
favorite horses race.

The horses were sleek, elegant, muscular, well-bred, and fast.
REAL FAST.

Except for one. His name was Seabiscuit. He loved to eat and sleep but hated to run. He had lost almost every race he had ever been in. His first trainer called him a "big dog."

Who would want a racehorse like that?

Charles Howard, that's who! He bought Seabiscuit for a bargain price. He thought the funny-looking animal had potential.

And so did these people. . . .

Charles Howard, Seabiscuit's owner

Howard became a millionaire by selling cars. He began his business when owning a car was quite unpopular. But he liked to take chances. It's no wonder he saw the potential in Seabiscuit!

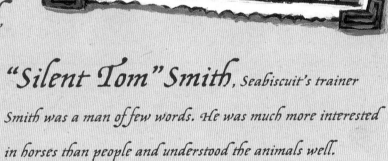

John "Red" Pollard,

Seabiscuit's jockey

"Silent Tom" Smith, Seabiscuit's trainer

Smith was a man of few words. He was much more interested in horses than people and understood the animals well.

Pollard was nicknamed "Red" because of his red hair. Finding work as a jockey was hard, so for extra money he boxed. In his free time he loved to read and recite poetry. He identified with troubled animals.

Seabiscuit was wild, but Silent Tom knew what was wrong—the small horse was lonely. In came some friends to calm him down.

Seabiscuit was lazy. Silent Tom knew the problem there, too—the horse needed motivation. So in came the competition!

Seabiscuit was angry and stubborn. Red Pollard knew how to fix that. He didn't punish the horse like so many others had done in the past. He showed 'Biscuit that he was his friend, not his enemy.

The once angry and wild horse became gentle. The once lazy horse became competitive and fast! But would anyone notice? After Seabiscuit won his first big race, people sure did!

Wow, a horse that looked just like them! Beat-up. Imperfect. An underdog. A horse with courage! Word traveled fast. People had "Seabiscuit-itis," described one sportswriter.

Even though Seabiscuit was becoming famous, there was another horse who was more so. His name was War Admiral. War Admiral was sleek, elegant, muscular, and fast.
REAL FAST.

Charles Howard wanted his horse to be the most famous, fastest horse in history, so he challenged War Admiral to a race. War Admiral's owner, Samuel Riddle, scoffed at the challenge. Mr. Riddle thought the goofy-looking challenger didn't compare to his grand horse. Could Seabiscuit beat War Admiral? People wondered.

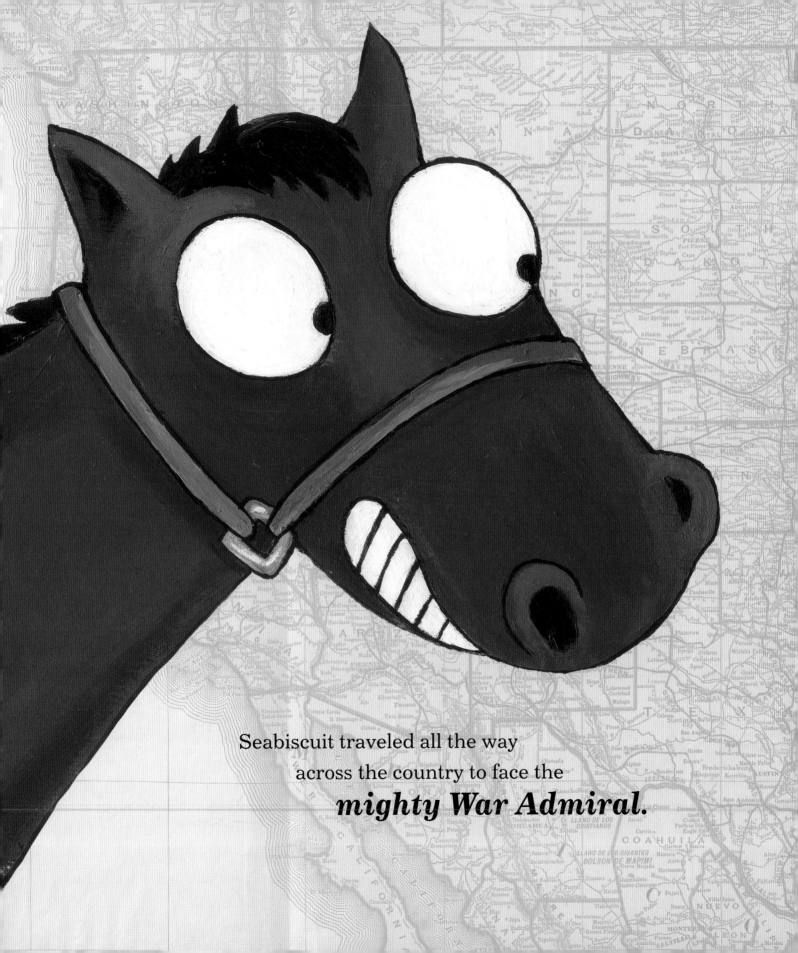

Seabiscuit traveled all the way
across the country to face the
mighty War Admiral.

Sadly an accident happened the day before the big race. Red Pollard was riding another horse, the horse got spooked, and Red went flying. Red's leg was badly injured and he was rushed to the hospital. He was told he'd never race again. Red was heartbroken. Everyone was disappointed. Was the race off?

No! From his hospital bed, Red asked his good friend George "The Iceman" Woolf to race in his place. **The race was on!**

Many people came to watch the race. By train. By car. By boat. By the thousands! They were squished—crammed in like sardines—but that didn't matter.

Jobs closed early so that no one would miss the race. Forty million Americans tuned in. Even President Roosevelt did!

Everyone nervously watched the empty racetrack.
In came War Admiral. In came Seabiscuit! A hush
fell over the crowd. The horses twitched.
The riders sat perfectly still.

"And they're off!" shouted the announcer. Seabiscuit took the early lead, but War Admiral was catching up fast!

"They're head-and-head. . . . It's the best horse from here in," proclaimed the announcer. Woolf whispered into Seabiscuit's ear. Then he turned to War Admiral and his rider. "So long, Charley!" he said. Like a freight train, 'Biscuit flew past War Admiral.

War Admiral tried to catch up—
but couldn't. Seabiscuit was too fast.

"Seabiscuit leads by a length," said
the announcer. "Now Seabiscuit by a
length and a half . . . Seabiscuit by three!"

**"Seabiscuit is the winner
by four lengths!"** shouted the
announcer. "And you never saw such
a wild crowd!"

Woolf rode 'Biscuit into the winner's circle to a roar of cheers and a burst of flashbulbs. "I wish my old pal Red was on him instead of me," Woolf said.

Seabiscuit was America's hero. **A LITTLE HORSE WITH THE HEART OF A LION**, proclaimed one newspaper. People were able to forget their troubles, even if just for a minute.

AUTHOR'S NOTE

Seabiscuit was a champion, but it was the loving determination of the team at Howard's barn that put him in the winner's circle.

Charles Howard got his start as a young entrepreneur by opening a bicycle repair shop. In the early 1900s the main forms of transportation were the horse and buggy, and bicycles. It wasn't until a distraught motor vehicle owner arrived in his shop seeking some repairs that Howard turned his attention to cars. First he fixed them and then he raced and sold them, making a fortune as a result. People traded in their horses to get a new car. Howard once said he "wouldn't give fifty dollars for the best horse living."

Unfortunately the cars that made Howard rich also broke his heart. His fifteen-year-old son, Frankie, died in a tragic accident while driving his father's truck. Howard never fully recovered. He opened a hospital in his son's name and left his love of cars behind. Howard turned his attention to horses, with a newfound interest in racing them. But before Howard could turn his horses into winners, he needed the right trainer.

Before becoming Howard's horse trainer, Tom Smith spent much time on the plains, alone, with his horse. The Indians called him the Lone Plainsman. By the time Smith had reached civilization he'd acquired the nickname Silent Tom. A witness claimed that after accidentally chopping off his toe, Smith jiggled it out of his boot and said only three words, "That's my toe." Whether this is true or not, it is clear Smith was a man of little words. "He nods hello, shakes hands good-bye, and hasn't said a hundred words in all," said one reporter. Smith was often caught making horse noises, blowing air in and out as horses do. "It's easy to talk to a horse if you understand his language," he said.

Smith was a man of the frontier, but the country was changing. People such as Howard were responsible for paving the road to civilization, and gone was the need for horses and horse trainers. But Howard needed him. Smith had a particular talent for knowing what animals were thinking. "Learn your horse. Each one is an individual, and once you penetrate his mind and heart, you can often work wonders with an otherwise intractable beast." Smith was the perfect man to turn the impossibly stubborn Seabiscuit into a winner. Now Howard needed the perfect jockey.

As a boy, Red Pollard dreamed of being a jockey and begged his parents to let him go to the racetracks. They let him go, but only if accompanied by a trusted family friend. Sadly Pollard's guardian abandoned him and at the age of fifteen he was left to fend for himself. He went from stall to stall, asking for a chance to ride. For spare change, Pollard also boxed under the nickname Cougar. His life was finally coming together. Pollard was winning and ranked number 12 in the racing circuit. But as the years went by, he won fewer and fewer races. It didn't help that Pollard was blind in the right eye—an injury that would have gotten him banned from racing if anyone knew his secret. By the time Tom Smith found him, Pollard was a losing jockey whom no one would hire. Red Pollard did have one amazing skill and Smith spotted it immediately. He was good with troubled animals and Seabiscuit was no exception. With one little sugar cube, Pollard won Seabiscuit over. He would become Seabiscuit's new jockey.

Every good story has a happy ending. Although Pollard did not race in the match against War Admiral on November 1, 1938, he did get his winning ride. Being the determined man that he was, Pollard ignored the doctor's claim that he'd never ride again. Although his leg was mangled, Pollard tried again and again to walk without the use of crutches. While he was recuperating at the Howard ranch, Seabiscuit joined him. The now-famous horse had incurred a leg injury of his own and was brought back to the ranch for everyone to fret over him. Most horses with a leg injury are put to sleep, but no one dared do it to Seabiscuit. So both Pollard and Seabiscuit hobbled together. "Seabiscuit and I were a couple of old cripples . . . all washed up," he said.

Their long walks on the ranch did the trick. "Among the hooting owls, we both got sound again." After months of recovery they were ready.

For Pollard and Seabiscuit, just being able to race again was a miracle, but what happened on March 2, 1940, was even more newsworthy. Seabiscuit raced across the wire to win the coveted Santa Anita Handicap. The "ugly duckling with the lame leg" and the "busted-down jockey" proved everyone wrong. They had won the hearts of America.

SOURCES

American Experience. "Seabiscuit: The Long Shot That Captured America's Heart." Dir. Stephen Ives. WGBH Educational Foundation, 2002.

———. "Seabiscuit: The Long Shot That Captured America's Heart." Available at: http://www.pbs.org/wgbh/amex/seabiscuit/. Accessed throughout 2006 through 2008.

Beckwith, B. K. *Seabiscuit: The Saga of a Great Champion.* Pennsylvania: Westholme Publishing, 2003.

Field, Bryan. "40,000 Watch Seabiscuit Defeat War Admiral at Pimlico" *New York Times*, 2 November 1938.

———. "Eastern Fans Pick War Admiral to Take $100,000 Race May 30" *New York Times*, 14 April 1938.

———. "War Admiral Will Meet Seabiscuit Today in Special Race for Championship" *New York Times*, 1 November 1938.

Hillenbrand, Laura. *Seabiscuit: An American Legend.* New York: Ballantine Books, 2001.

McEvoy, John. *The Seabiscuit Story: From the Pages of the Nation's Most Prominent Racing Magazine.* Lexington: Eclipse Press, 2003.

New York Times, "C. S. Howard Sr., 70, Seabiscuit Owner." 7 June 1950.

———, "Jockey Pollard is Hurt." 24 June 1938.

———, "Jockey Pollard Retires." 31 March 1940.

———, "Match Seabiscuit with War Admiral." *New York Times*, 6 October 1938.

———, "Seabiscuit 'Best in World.'" 2 November 1938.

Seabiscuit: The Lost Documentary. Dir. Manny Nathan Hahn. Legend Films, 1939.

Seabiscuit vs. War Admiral—1938 Match Race. Available at http://www.youtube.com/watch?v=WVT2MPNCqgM&feature=related. Accessed throughout 2007 and 2008.

Time, "The Cougar Calls It Quits." January 9, 1956, http://www.time.com/time/magazine/article/0,9171,866734,00.html.

———, "Four Hundred Grand." March 11, 1940, http://www.time.com/time/magazine/article/0,9171,789679,00.html.

———, "Man o' Warriors." November 14, 1938, http://www.time.com/time/magazine/article/0,9171,772063,00.html.

———, "Seasoned Biscuit." May 9, 1938, http://www.time.com/time/magazine/article/0,9171,759606,00.html.